Carb Cycli

Shredding, Muscle Building

Meals Which Will Eliminate

Your Skinnyfat Physique

Forever

The following eBook is reproduced below with the goal of providing information that is as accurate and reliable as possible. Regardless, purchasing this eBook can be seen as consent to the fact that both the publisher and the author of this book are in no way experts on the topics discussed within and that any recommendations or suggestions that are made herein are for entertainment purposes only. Professionals should be consulted as needed prior to undertaking any of the action endorsed herein.

This declaration is deemed fair and valid by both the American Bar Association and the Committee of Publishers Association and is legally binding throughout the United States.

Furthermore, the transmission, duplication or reproduction of any of the following work including specific information will be considered an illegal act irrespective of if it is done electronically or in print. This extends to creating a secondary or tertiary copy of the work or a recorded copy and is only allowed with an expressed written consent from the Publisher. All additional right reserved.

The information in the following pages is broadly considered to be a truthful and accurate account of facts and as such any inattention, use or misuse of the information in question by the reader will render any resulting actions solely under their purview. There are no scenarios in which the publisher or the original author of this work can be in any fashion deemed liable for any hardship or damages that may befall them after undertaking information described herein.

Additionally, the information in the following pages is intended only for informational purposes and should thus be thought of as universal. As befitting its nature, it is presented without assurance regarding its prolonged validity or interim quality. Trademarks that are mentioned are done without written consent and can in no way be considered an endorsement from the trademark holder.

Medical Disclaimer

This book is not intended as a substitute for the medical advice of physicians. The reader should regularly consult a physician in matters relating to his/her health and particularly with respect to any symptoms that may require diagnosis or medical attention.

Please consult your physician before starting any diet or exercise program.
Any recommendations given in this book are not a substitute for medical advice.

Contents

Contents..4

Introduction.. 5

The Science Behind Carb Cycling.................................. 8

    Why Carb-Cycling is Neccesary for Your Fitness Goals..13

    Carb Cycling for Stubborn Fat Loss....................... 16

Optimal Workout Routines for Carb Cycling...............19

How to Calculate Your Calorie Intake for Carb Cycling39

The Two Carb Cycling Protocols....................................41

    The Two Step Method...42

    The 3 Step Method...47

Carb Cycling Recipes.. 51

    15 Minute No-Hassle Breakfasts...........................51

        Low Carb Day...51

        High Carb Day..56

    Main Meals..60

        Low Carb Day...60

        High Carb Day..75

    Snacks & Desserts...85

        Low Carb Day...85

        High Carb Day..92

What to Do When Your Weight Loss Stalls.................97

Conclusion...101

Other Books by Jason Michaels.................................. 104

Introduction

Hello and welcome to *Carb Cycling Recipes: Fat Shredding, Muscle Building Recipes Which Will Eliminate Your Skinnyfat Physique Forever*

I'm Jason, and the following chapters will discuss how and why carb cycling is your solution to stubborn fat loss, lean bulking and transforming your life forever. As a former "skinnyfat" person myself, I know first hand just how difficult weight loss can be for someone in your position. This applies to women just as much as it does to men. You've probably tried a bunch of diets in the past like keto, paleo or whatever the latest Men's Health flavour of the month is. This is not a diet in the strict sense of the word in that there are "forbidden foods" or "cheat days". So you won't be following for a limited time until you reach your goal and then quit. Rather it's a true lifestyle change focused on the foundational principles of providing stable energy, and adequate vitamins, the correct amino acids essential fatty acids, minerals, fiber, and defensive anti-inflammatory phytonutrients to reach and maintain your fitness goals

If this all sounds complicated to right now, don't worry. We'll break down any unfamiliar terminology in the coming chapters. We'll also be discussing the science behind carb cycling, and just why it works wonders if you're coming from a position where weight loss hasn't always been easy for you. Once equipped with this understanding, you'll learn what you can do about it with targeted goals based on your macronutrient needs (don't worry - we'll show you how to find those out as well). As well as how to consume less processed and fast foods and more fresh whole foods including plenty of fruits and vegetables.

This book also navigates through and beyond misinformation and myths surrounding various diet protocols and lays the groundwork for your new lifestyle. We'll also be looking over training plans, and how to set up one which works for you, one which you can stick to, and one which works regardless of your experience (or lack of) in the gym itself.

There are plenty of books on this subject on the market, thanks again for choosing this one! Every effort was made to ensure it is full of as much useful information as possible, please enjoy!

Thanks,

Jason

The Science Behind Carb

Cycling

While carb cycling has long been a time-tested strategy used by bodybuilders and physique competitors for both getting stage ready and staying lean in the offseason when they are trying to put on muscle mass, it's previously been off the radar of the mainstream fitness community. This mainstream community has often favored low carb approaches like the ketogenic diet for example.

However, in recent years, there have been a number of scientific studies which prove that carb cycling isn't just something which huge muscle bound bodybuilders can benefit from. There are scientific benefits for the average Joe or Jane who just wants to look and feel better.

So no, we're not talking about broscience here, we're talking about real science. In this chapter, we'll be discussing the actual science behind what effects carb cycling actually has on your body.

Carb cycling is born out of the principle of adjusting your carbohydrate intake based on your activity level on that particular day. By doing this, you maintain a healthy metabolism while keeping your performance inside the gym as high as possible.

The main problem which "skinnyfat" people have with weight loss, is that they find their weight loss tends to plateau quicker than others. This can be disheartening and demotivating, and as such, they tend to give up on their diets quicker than others.

Fortunately, adjusting your carb intake like this can help you break through these plateaus quickly, because it allows your body to utilize certain fat loss hormones like insulin.

By spiking your carb intake with a high carb day, you elevate your insulin levels which then optimizes their anabolic effects.

This also has the beneficial effects of helping control hunger.

You still follow general nutrition rules of utilizing a calorie surplus for muscle gain and a calorie deficit for fat loss.

The difference with carb cycling, as opposed to a normal deficit, is that your overall calorie intake differs on training days and rest days.

Simply put, you eat more on training days in the form of increased carb intake, and then you eat less on rest days in the form of a lower carb intake.

For most people, I've found that to keep things as simple as possible for them, carbs are the only thing you need to change in your diet.

Others like to play around with fat intake as well, but I personally like to keep things as simple as possible for people. Because the easier a diet is to follow, the more likely you are to stick to it. That goes for any diet by the way, not just carb cycling.

In terms of studies done on a carb cycling protocol. One by Michelle Harvey, PhD showed that a carb cycling diet produced an 80% increase in fat loss versus a regular calorie controlled "healthy diet". A similar study conducted where carb cycling was put against the ketogenic diet yielded similar results.

I'd also make a point that keto diet tends to favor "front end" weight loss more because of their restrictive nature. Whereas carb cycling can be more useful in a long-term setting.

In terms of athletic performance, a study *Medicine in Sports Science and Exercise* by Marguet et al (2016) on two groups of triathletes showed that the group who ate a carb cycling diet showed increased performance in both cycling and running when compared to a group who ate a regular diet. Interestingly enough, this included training sessions where they were in a "low carb" state, which indicates that the age old adage of "more carbs = better workouts" may not be as simple of a conclusion as we would have previously thought.

Why Carb-Cycling is Neccesary for Your Fitness Goals

So. How do we carb cycle? Well here is a simple rule:

A. Take in carbs on days when you work out.

B. Remove them from your diet when you don't.

I'll be discussing specific protocols later on in the book, but that is pretty much the gist of it.

The role of protein in a carb cycling diet

Protein is still the single most important nutrient for maintaining and gaining muscle. Carb cycling doesn't change that.

The Recommended Daily Allowance is generally between 60-80g a day. While this will generally keep you free from disease and ensure your body functions properly in a day-to-day setting, it is far too low if you want to accomplish any sort of fitness related goals.

As a general rule of thumb, 1g of protein for every pound of muscle mass is an easy guideline to follow. So if you're a 180lb male, you should be aiming to consume 180g of protein a day. For females, I recommend the same amount, although you can get away with 0.8g protein per lb.

I do not subscribe to some of the outdated bodybuilding conventions of 2 or even 3g of protein per pound of body weight. I feel these are designed to shill protein powder supplements more than anything else (because otherwise, how are people eating 350g-400g of protein a day?)

Where should your protein come from?

I won't go too in depth with this subject, because realistically that could be a whole other book. But sticking to whole food sources like eggs, beef, chicken, fish, tuna, cheese and milk is your best bet.

I'm not fundamentally opposed to protein powders, and having 1 scoop of whey a day isn't as bad as others would make it out to be, but I would not rely on it as your main source of protein. I once heard of a certain bodybuilder who consumed 90% of his protein in the form of shakes because he just "didn't like meat that much" and apart from being intrigued by what his bowel movements must be like, I just thought what a poor diet that must be from an amino acid and micronutrient perspective. So yeah, protein powders can be part of your diet, but only a small part.

For vegans and vegetarians, they may need to make up a larger part of your overall protein intake, but I still recommend focusing on whole foods first and foremost.

Carb Cycling for Stubborn Fat Loss

Carb cycling can also be a useful tool for stubborn fat loss. This is when you've already lost a decent amount of weight, but still find areas or pockets of fat on various parts of your body. These differ between men and women but are often in the following places.

- Lower abs
- Inner thighs
- Lower chest
- Lower back (love handles)

If you're experiencing this, then don't worry, this is perfectly normal. That's because not all body fat is stored in your body the same way.

For example, visceral fat is fat stored around your organs like your liver or stomach (this is why men tend to get beer bellies). Visceral fat is easy to burn, which is why belly fat is often the first to go when men go on a diet.

Subcutaneous fat is the kind of fat we're dealing with in a stubborn fat scenario. This is the kind of fat which stored underneath your skin. Women have a lot more of this than men (which is why women always have naturally higher body fat percentages). These fat deposits build up over time, and are the last to go away with a diet. This is then compounded by the fact that these are the areas on our body which have the worst blood flow (and we need blood flow to burn fat). Once again, women have a harder time because more of their fat is stored in low blood flow areas like thighs and hips.

Ok, enough of the bad news, what can carb cycling do to remove these stubborn fat cells?

Remember when we discussed insulin earlier, and how high carb days can boost our insulin response, which is great for muscle building. Well, insulin is bad when you have these excess fat cells, and that's where our low carb days come in. By having lower insulin levels, your fat cells are more "primed" to be burned, and in turn, you will store less fat. That's how carb cycling can be super effective in a fat burning scenario.

Optimal Workout Routines

for Carb Cycling

Losing weight is a process that involves three major factors; nutrition, training and rest. Striking the correct balance between this triumvirate is key to maximizing results; you can't out-train a bad diet in the same way that poor nutrition will not allow proper development of muscle tissue if you're not getting enough protein in your daily meals. The simple calculus is this; calories in versus calories out. If you're expending more calories than you take in, you will be in a calorific deficit and therefore, lose weight. The opposite is also true, eat more food than your body needs and it will lead to weight gain, through new muscle tissue and fat cells.

Our goals are of course to reduce body fat and obtain an overall more aesthetically pleasing look. This is where smart training comes in to play. I say smart because it's key to differentiate between training "hard" and training smart. It's something I've been guilty of and that's why I'm not afraid to say that training like a moron will impact your goals. Ask yourself this; if you head into every workout attempting to hit every body part, using as much equipment as possible and taking every set to failure, do you think that's training smart? It's not, and it will be to the detriment of your development.

However, walking into the gym, lifting a weight that's easy to move and doesn't tax you for about 3 sets of 8 reps and repeating this with maybe 2 or 3 exercises will equally see minimal progress, if any. Therefore, the optimal training regime will leave you feeling the workout, yet not feeling like a completely broken down individual. We'll be covering the intricate details of an optimal training regime to bring about the best results for crafting the ultimate physique by promoting fat loss as well as muscle gain.

Rest

Before we get down to the specifics of a training session in terms of what to lift and how to lift it, let's circle back to the concept of resting. I know exactly what it's like to have so much energy and motivation that taking a day off seems preposterous, but the fact is, if you don't rest, your body doesn't repair and therefore muscle tissue won't develop and as such, you'll lose out on those all-important gains. The rule of thumb that I've lived by is to ensure you're working out at least 3 days in the week. During those 3 days, you can target multiple muscle groups and then use the days off to recover effectively, before attacking that first body part you hit. In practice it would look similar to this;

Monday

Legs

Tuesday

Rest

Wednesday

Shoulders and Arms

Thursday

Rest

Friday

Chest and Back

Saturday

Rest

Sunday

Legs

In this example, you would progress through the days, hitting the various body parts in the same order and therefore ensuring everything is worked out at least twice within a 7 day period, which assures a high level of growth is maintained, whilst not overtraining. Overtraining can lead to injuries and higher fatigue levels, which in the long term drives motivation through the floor as you'll be far too tired to even want to go to the gym, much less prepare a good meal that hits all of your macronutrients. Overtraining can be a real momentum killer, so don't fall into the trap of thinking a rest is going to block your progress; it won't.

Rest times within the gym also need to be paid attention to. With the goal of fat loss and muscle growth in mind, we're not going to be taking 3-5 minute rest intervals between sets. We're not power lifting here or going for one rep maximum lifts on the squat rack; 90 seconds will be the maximum time allowed before getting back to the set. Your heart should be beating fast and sweat should be forming on your forehead; the body needs to be in that fat-burning state with blood pumping and everything working.

Set Number and Rep Range

Here's where things get interesting. One question you'll likely have is "how many sets of this exercise do I do and how many reps should be done in each set?" Follow up questions will include "should I go to failure every time? What about drop sets and supersets? What even are they? Come to think of it, what is a set and what is a rep?" As you can see, in a tiny timeframe, a can of worms has been opened and there's a myriad of questions spilling forth. First of all, take a breath and relax. It's not as complicated as people like to make it out to be, so don't fret.

Let's take a look at some of the terminology used above. Beginning with "reps" which is short for repetitions, this defines the number of times you perform a particular exercise. So, therefore, if you complete 12 reps this will equal one set, so in practice 4 sets of 10-12 reps will mean you complete an exercise (bench press for example) 10 times on 4 occasions. Rest time (which as explained earlier will be limited to 90 seconds) will separate sets. You may be wondering if you jump straight into lifting as heavy and as hard as you can and to this, I say, sure, if you're looking for an injury.   To prevent this from occurring, it's vital you warm up appropriately on each exercise, before diving into the working sets. A "working set" is where the sets will "count" - i.e. if you are due to complete 4 sets, it will be these working sets that count, not the warm-up sets before. Typically, it would take 2 sets to effectively warm up and you should increase the weight incrementally until you hit something that is a challenge to obtain the 12 or so reps.   Here's how it would look in practice;

Exercise - Barbell Bench Press

Warm up set 1 - 20kg - 20 reps

Warm up set 2 - 40kg - 15- 20 reps

Working set 1 - 60kg - 12- 15 reps

Working set 2 - 60kg 12-15 reps

Working set 3 - 60kg 12-15 reps

Working set 4 - 60kg 12-15 reps

The goal here is to ensure you stay in that 12-15 rep range for each working set. On Set 1, you might hit the 15 reps quite comfortably (note, if it's too easy, increase the weight or reps). However, Set 2 might be more of a challenge and you could get 15, but at a struggle. By Set 4, your body part (in this case, the chest) will be screaming and you'll barely make it to the 12 reps. If you can keep this thought in mind, you'll be doing the correct amount of work to promote muscle growth and fat loss. What we want to avoid is taking each set to failure.

Failure, as the name implies, is where you simply cannot go any further and not even a single rep can be forced out. While this is something we would be looking to achieve with the last set of each exercise, it's redundant to make this a regular occurrence throughout each set. You see, what happens when the body gets close to failure is rep quality quickly diminishes. Taking the example of barbell bench press again, the closer you get to failure, you are more likely to "half-rep" and not get a full range of movement throughout each rep. It's a normal reaction to do this, especially if you are training alone as your brain will naturally be trying to protect you from hurting yourself, so the full range of movement is reduced because your brain thinks "it may not be possible for you to get the weight back up off your chest, let's be careful". In practice, it's unlikely this will ever happen and indeed, there will always be someone around to assist you with your lifting. So, taking the information above about a half-rep and not generating the full range of movement with each lift, this means the body parts involved are not achieving the maximum potential for growth and in the long run, you can end up with underdeveloped aspects of your physique compared with other areas of your muscular structure which you have been training efficiently. It goes back to the initial declaration of training smart rather than foolishly. Put the ego to one side and instead of focusing on what number is written on the side of the plate, look at the bigger picture and as long as the weight is a challenge for you, that's all that matters.

Supersets and dropsets add further layers of depth to your training and serve as an excellent addition to any program. Beginning with a superset, this is where two exercises will be combined, back to back to form one set. Typically it will be two smaller muscle groups working opposite sides of the body. One example will be completing a set of barbell curls and then immediately going to tricep pushdowns using a rope attachment on the cable machine. These two exercises will target the biceps and triceps respectively and have the whole arm nicely pumped and fatigued! The effect of this is two-fold; firstly it keeps the body working and in the fat-burning state, which is exactly where we want to be. Secondly, it's also a time saver, which is an important consideration. While it is again subjective, spending over 90 minutes in the gym tips into the realm of being unnecessary, as typically you can complete an intense weight session within 60 minutes (including stretching, which we'll get to) and then spend 30 minutes on cardiovascular exercise. Anything longer and you have to question once again if you're training smart.

Stretching

Speaking of smart, it's imperative that you stretch. This should be done after your weight session and should focus on the body part you've just trained. So after a chest workout, get over to an area where you can perform stretching with lots of space. Stretching is so vital to your body, yet often overlooked. First and foremost, a good stretch ensures that you'll be reducing the risk of injury, as the tight muscles can seize up, whereas the act of stretching will lengthen the muscles just used. This has the secondary benefit of helping growth in a certain area. If your chest muscle is extremely tight and you don't stretch, it will never be fully opened up and therefore you won't get the full muscle development desired.

Cardiovascular Exercise

Some people love it, some hate it, but cardiovascular exercises (termed "cardio" for short) are an imperative part of any training package, but particularly for weight loss. Any form of cardio will work the heart and circulatory system, which means increased blood flow throughout your body enabling sustained movement. Once again, cardio is not simply jumping on a treadmill and smashing into a run at 100 miles an hour for 20 minutes before turning the machine off; once again we're going to be approaching this in the correct way, the smart way.

Firstly, there are two types of cardio; High-intensity interval training (HIIT) and Low-intensity steady state (LISS), both of which need be employed in order to maximize fat loss and actually improve overall health. Let's start with LISS and why this is important.

In a nutshell, your body begins to use oxygen for energy inside the muscular system after 2 minutes. Aerobic or LISS exercise can last from 10 minutes all the way up to 2 hours by using this oxygenated blood to transfer energy to the working muscles. If we look at running as the example, a long distance run or marathon training is a perfect example of aerobic exercise. The key is to keep the intensity low, so it's not going to be sprinting for 30 minutes, but rather a pace just above a jog. LISS is excellent for generating increased energy, better blood flow and a stronger heart. Take caution, however, as only using LISS as your cardio outlet will not burn fat in the long run. In fact, your body will become used to the process and you'll simply have to run longer and further in order to get a minimal amount of gain and this is why we also need to make use of HIIT to prevent cardio plateau and keep the body guessing.

HIIT is the other side of the same coin, in that it's still cardio, but it's a variation of the steady state. With HIIT, the anaerobic system is used, which is all about short bursts of intense exercise lasting anywhere from 15 seconds to 2 minutes. As opposed to oxygen being used, the body will use its glycogen resource as the energy source. So that's the Science part out of the way, why is this useful for you and your fat loss goals? Simply put, it's an extremely effective way to burn calories and it carries over to when you sleep as well. That's right, you'll be burning calories while you snooze, which is why it's important to get adequate amounts of rest. Another important benefit from HIIT is that your metabolism gets a boost. This means your body will be efficiently processing the food you eat, resulting in no excess fat being stored. HIIT, as the name suggests is quite intense, which is why it shouldn't be performed every day and rather in conjunction with LISS to maximize the fat burning and calorie depletion and yet keep your body in a good shape and free from the effects of burning out. Once more, it's about training intelligently in order to get the most out of your training sessions. An example of a HIIT workout could be conducted on a static cycling machine and you cycle at a steady pace, low intensity setting for 45 seconds and then increase the resistance on the machine and sprint for 15 seconds, before again lowering resistance and pace for 45 seconds.

In conjunction with the above cardio exercises, it's also important to be mindful of how many steps you are completing every day. Again, another form of LISS, walking gives the body another outlet to burn calories, get the blood pumping and keep your heart nice and strong. Step count will vary from person to person, but if you have a desk-based office job, for example, it's fairly unlikely you'll be getting many steps in at all. Therefore, a good target should be 10,000 steps a day initially, as this will take your body from a sedated state to an active one. Tracking steps doesn't mean you count in your head every time you walk, there are plenty of neat gadgets you can use to make this easier for you such as apps for your Smartphone or a Fit Bit you can wear on your wrist. If you have a dog, then getting the steps in whilst walking with your canine companion should be a fun way to rack up the numbers, but even if you don't have a pet you can use an excuse to go for a walk, you can simply take a leisurely stroll to clear your head, take a breather and escape from everything for a short while.

Now that we have the principles of training in place, it's almost time to delve into what an example routine would look like. But just before that, I'll briefly touch upon the value of a training partner. Now again, it's important to be training with someone who trains smart and has similar goals to you. As we'll be aiming to burn fat and increase muscle tone, training with your 250lbs power-lifting friend will likely not be conducive to your personal goals. In an ideal world, you'll find someone with a similar physique to yours (or even slightly better) who trains at the same time of day you do and has matching, if not the same aspirations for where they want to take their body. A good training partner can really help push you on in sessions where you want to throw in the towel and you'll find that extra rep you need can be reached with a little encouragement either mentally or physically through a good spot. However, training alone also has its benefits. There's a lot to be said for sticking in your headphones, pumping your favorite tunes and shutting out the whole world. I've personally trained alone for several years and found it was a therapeutic way to get the working day out of my system and give me that much needed alone time. Finally, you may be wondering what time of day you should train? The honest answer is that it doesn't matter and instead will revolve around your lifestyle and preferences. Personally, I train at 5:30am simply because it gets my day off to a flying start before work and I can have my entire evening free to myself. However, you may prefer to train after work at 5pm, or even later in the evening at 8:30pm. There's no right or wrong answer here, it will solely depend on you and what fits in with your schedule.

Training Example

Chest and Back

Exercise	Number of Reps	Number of Sets
Incline Barbell Press	12-15	4
Wide Lat-Pulldown	10-12	4
Flat Dumbbell Press	10-12	4
Bent Over Row	8-12	3
Cable Machine Fly	12-15	3
Seated Row	12-15	4
Superset – Landmine Hex Press with T-Bar Row	10-12	3 sets of each = 6 sets in total

Cardio – HIIT

20 Minutes total
Static Cycling Machine
45 Seconds Steady State – Low Resistance
15 Seconds Sprint – Higher Resistance

As you can see, this session will include a high amount of sets (28 in total) and reps that will lead to your body being in a consistent fat burning phase. The addition of HIIT after the workout will have your calorie expenditure high and thus fat loss being the key benefit.

Final Thoughts

Training doesn't need to be complicated or a chore. When you look at the 3 aspects of crafting the physique of your dreams, training should be the fun part. Rest and nutrition are essentials that must be looked after carefully, but working out is where you can be free, enjoy the process and form bonds with like-minded individuals. If you train hard 3 days a week,

I promise you, you'll see results. Have fun with the journey, be smart and most importantly, be consistent. Don't let a bad day at the office steer you off the path of glory, stick with the plan, keep your head down and reap the rewards.

How to Calculate Your Calorie

Intake for Carb Cycling

Like with any diet, you should leave nothing to chance and instead focus on tracking your food and calorie intake as much as possible. But in order to do that accurately, you need to an accurate starting point.

In order to do this, you need to work out your **Basal Metabolic Rate (or BMR)**. This takes into account your normal calorie levels based on your height and weight, and then also factors in your activity levels.

The formula gives you a base level calorie amount, which assumes you do zero physical activity that day (e.g. if you lay in bed for 24 hours), and then an actual amount based on your activity level.

For example, if you are a 32 year old female, who stands at 5'4 (162cm) and weighs 141lbs (62kg) and goes to the gym 3 times a week.

Then your BMR would be 2,1966 calories, this is the amount of calories you would need to maintain your current weight based on your current activity level.

To calculate your BMR easily, I recommend using this website https://www.thecalculatorsite.com/health/bmr-calculator.php

Note, for those who of you who are training, I recommend the Harris-Benedict formula as opposed to the traditional Mifflin-St. Jeor formula.

Don't worry too much how your calorie intake will differ on different days because I'll be discussing that in greater depth in a later chapter. For now, just calculate your BMR because you'll be needing it going forward.

The Two Carb Cycling

Protocols

Before we begin, I should note that In this section I'll include a sample carb cycling schedule for both fat loss and muscle gain.

There are two main carb cycling protocols you can use.

The two step method and the three step method.

The two step method has 2 different calories intakes, a high carb day and a low carb day.

The three step method has 3, a high carb day, a medium carb day, and a low carb day.

We'll cover the two step method first.

For both methods we will use the guidelines discussed in the previous chapter of 1g protein per pound of bodyweight and then dietary fat of 30% of total calorie intake. This leaves us enough room to adequately cycle our carb intake.

The Two Step Method

For Fat Loss

Let's say you train 3 times a week, so you'll be eating your maintenance calories on training days, and then 700 calories below your maintenance on off days.

On your training days you'll eat 2,850 calories and on your rest days, you'll eat 2,150 calories.

This gives you a net deficit of 2,800 calories which is near a pound a week of fat loss.

To give a quick sample overview, this is what a typical training day would look like

Typical Training Day

2,850 calories

190g protein

375g carbs

65g fat

Breakfast/meal 1:

3 medium eggs - scrambled

2 cups brown rice

30g scoop whey protein with water

100g mixed berries

Lunch:

8oz chicken breast cooked in olive or coconut oil

3 large sweet potatoes

200g green beans

Dinner:

6oz beef sirloin or 80/20 ground beef

3 cups mashed potatoes

150g steamed broccoli

1 apple

Post-workout meal (taken as appropriate when you train):

2 cups grape juice

30g protein powder

Typical Rest Day

2,150 calories

190g protein

75g carbs

120g fat

Breakfast:

6 eggs scrambled

150g spinach

75g mixed berries

1 apple

Lunch:

8oz chicken thighs

300g mixed salad leaves with vinaigrette/olive oil

75g mixed berries

Dinner:

8oz beef sirloin

1 small sweet potato

Steamed broccoli

For Muscle Gain

Now for muscle gain your typical carb cycle would be +300 calories on training days and then maintenance calories on off days. This will ensure that you gain less muscle, without putting on the excess fat which a lot of natural athletes end up doing during their bulk cycles.

The 3 Step Method

As previously mentioned, this method requires three difficult carb intakes throughout the week.

A high carb has on this protocol is anything with above 200g of carbs.
A medium carb day is between 100 and 200g of carbs.
A low carb day is less than 50g of carbs (note: this is not the same as ketosis, you will not go into a ketogenic state on a carb cycling plan).

This particular method is more geared towards fat loss, as the significantly lower carb intake on lower carb days makes it trickier to use in a muscle gain protocol.

For a typical week, you will have 2 high carb days, 2 medium carb days and 3 low carb days.

Let's assume you're a 170lb male in your late twenties with light activity level. Your BMR will be around 2350 calories

You high carb days will be at maintenance, your medium carb days will be -300 calories and your low carb days will be -600 calories. This sets you up for a net calorie deficit of 2400 for the week.

So high carb - 2350 calories

Medium carb - 2050 calories

Low carb - 1750 calories

High carb macros:

170g protein

260g carbs

70g fat (30% of daily calories)

Medium carb macros:

170g protein

185g carbs

70g fat

Low carb macros:

170g protein

40g carbs

100g fat (increase to compensate for very low carbs)

Once again, let's assume you train 3 times a week, this would be how you set up your schedule.

Monday: Training day - High Carbs

Tuesday: Training day - Medium Carbs

Wednesday: Rest day - Low Carbs

Thursday: Training day - High Carbs

Friday: Training (if 4X per week) or Rest day - Medium Carbs

Saturday: Rest day - Low Carbs

Sunday: Rest day - Low Carbs

Running a protocol like this not only helps you get really lean, it also helps keep performance in the gym at an adequate level, because your high carbs will help your body performance on your medium carb training days (because there will still be excess glycogen left in your muscles from the day before.

The three step method also tends to work well for women in my experience.

Carb Cycling Recipes

15 Minute No-Hassle Breakfasts

Low Carb Day

Mixed berry smoothie

Total Prep & Cooking Time: 5 minutes

Yields: 1 Serving

Nutrition Facts (per serving)

Net Carbs: 7 g

Protein: 7.4 g (32.4g with protein powder)

Fats: 41 g

Calories: 400 (500 with protein powder)

What to Use

- Ice cubes (6)
- Your choice of sweetener (to taste)
- Coconut milk (.3 c)
- Mixed berries (.5 c frozen)
- Water (.5 c)
- Extra virgin olive oil (1 T)
- Optional: 1 scoop protein powder of your choice

Instructions

- Cream the coconut milk: This is a simple process. All you need to do is place the can of coconut milk in the refrigerator overnight. The next morning, open the can and spoon out the coconut milk that has solidified. Don't shake the can before opening. Discard the liquids.
- Add all of the ingredients, save the ice cubes, to the blender and blend on a low speed until pureed. Thin with water as needed.

- Add in the ice cubes and blend until the smoothie reaches your desired consistency.

Shakshuka

Total Prep & Cooking Time: 45 minutes

Yields: 4 Servings

Nutrition Facts (per serving)

- Protein: 26.1 g
- Net Carbs: 4.5 g
- Fats: 41.6 g
- Calories: 571

What to Use

- Eggs (5)
- Pepper (as desired)
- Salt (as desired)
- Chili powder (.25 tsp.)
- Paprika (1 tsp.)
- Cumin powder (1 tsp.)

- Tomatoes (1.5 chopped)
- Bell pepper (.5 chopped)
- Serrano pepper (.25 chopped)
- Garlic (1.5 cloves chopped)
- White onion (.5 chopped)
- Ghee (2 T)

Instructions

- Add the ghee to a skillet before placing it on the stove over a medium heat and adding in the onion. Let it cook for approximately 10 minutes, stirring consistently until it begins to soften.
- Add in the serrano pepper along with the garlic and let them cook for 2 minutes before adding in the red bell pepper and turning the heat to low. Let all the ingredients cook an additional 10 minutes, stirring consistently.
- Mix in the tomatoes and the remaining spices before letting the dish simmer and continue

cooking until the sauce has reduced to your desired level.

- •Add the eggs to the skillet before seasoning as desired and letting everything cook, covered for approximately 5 minutes until the eggs reach your desired level of doneness

High Carb Day

Whole wheat pancakes

Total Prep & Cooking Time: 50 minutes

Yields: 4 Servings

Nutrition Facts (per serving)

- Protein: 17 g
- Carbs: 85.3 g
- Fats: 29.6 g
- Calories: 548

What to Use

- Sea salt (1 tsp)
- Unsalted butter (5.3 T + 3 T)
- Eggs (2 beaten)
- Buttermilk (2.5 c)
- Brown sugar (2 T)
- Baking soda (.5 tsp)

- Baking powder (1.5 tsp)

- Wheat germ (.3 c)

- All-purpose flour (.6 c)

- Whole wheat flour (1 c)

- Raspberries (as desired)

- Optional: 1 scoop protein powder of your choice

Instructions

- Add the salt, brown sugar, baking soda, baking powder, wheat germ, flour and whole wheat flour to a food processor and process well.

- Add in the butter in small chunks to promote blending and process until the results have a consistency resembling sand.

- Create a well in the center of the results before adding in the eggs and buttermilk and mixing until all the liquids have been combined.

- Add 1 T oil to the skillet before adding the pan to the stove on top of a burner turned to a medium heat. Add enough batter to the skillet to form a 4 in. pancake. Cook each side for about 2 minutes, you will know it is time to flip them when you see a bubble start to form on the first side of the batter.

- Garnish with raspberries

Purple smoothie

Total Prep & Cooking Time: 5 minutes

Yields: 1 Serving

Nutrition Facts (per serving)

Calories 330

Total Carbohydrates 95 g

Protein 8 g

Total Fat 5 g

What to Use

- Banana (2)
- Orange (2, peeled)

- Organic mixed berries (1.5 c)
- Vanilla Greek Yogurt   (6 oz.)
- Ice Cubes (6)

Instructions

- Add all of the ingredients, save the ice cubes, to the blender and blend on a low speed until pureed. Thin with water as needed.
- Add in the ice cubes and blend until the smoothie reaches your desired consistency.

Main Meals

Low carb

Fish Pie

Total Prep & Cooking Time: 95 minutes

Yields: 6 Servings

Nutrition Facts (per serving)

- Fiber 4.2 g
- Carbohydrates (in total): 9.8 g
- Fats: 46.5 g
- Protein: 33.4 g
- Calories: 615

What to Use

- Salt (as needed)
- Pepper (as needed)
- Parsley (as garnish)

- Chives (4 T chopped)
- Cheddar cheese (1 c shredded)
- Nutmeg (.25 tsp.)
- Dijon mustard (1 tsp.)
- Water (.5 c)
- Heavy whipping cream (1 c)
- Cloves (.25 tsp. ground)
- Bay leaves (2)
- Red onion (1 sliced)
- Mackerel (2 filets skinless)
- Salmon (2 filets skinless)
- Haddock (2 filets skinless)
- Ghee (.25 c + 2 T)
- Cauliflower (1 chopped)
- Eggs (4)

Instructions

- Fill a pot with water and a pinch of salt before adding in the eggs and placing it on top of a burner turned to a high heat. After the water boils, remove the pot from the burner and let the eggs cook for 10 minutes.

- Once they are finished cooking, add the eggs to a bowl of cold water to prevent them from over cooking.

- Add a steaming rack to a pot that contains about 2 inches of water. Place the pot on top of a burner turned to high heat and let the water boil before letting the cauliflower steam for 10 minutes. Add the results to a blender along with the .25 c of ghee. Blend thoroughly.

- Dice all of the fish into manageable chunks and add them all to a deep pan before adding in the water and the cream. Add in the cloves, bay leaves and onions and mix well. Let the pot boil and then reduce the temperature to allow it to simmer about 8 minutes.

- Place the fish into the slow cooker after lining it with tinfoil.

- Add the rest of the butter and nutmeg to the fish sauce and let it continue to simmer for another 5 minutes until it thickens. Turn off the burner, remove the bay leaves and add in the cheddar cheese.

Stuffed flank steak

Total Prep & Cooking Time: 65 minutes

Yields: 6 Servings

Nutrition Facts (per serving)

- Protein: 54 g
- Net Carbs: 3 g
- Fats: 25 g
- Calories: 470

What to Use

- Pepper (as desired)
- Salt (as desired)
- Onion powder (.5 tsp.)
- Garlic powder (.5 tsp.)
- Egg yolk (1)
- Almond flour (2 T)
- Bleu cheese (4 oz.)
- Roasted peppers (7 oz. sliced)
- Spinach (16 oz.)

- Flank steak (2)

What to Do

- Ensure you are working with the steak from front to back before beginning to butterfly it, moving from right to left.
- Combine the rest of the ingredients and mix thoroughly in a large mixing bowl.
- Cover the steak in the mixture from the bowl and roll it up as tightly as possible before wrapping it in kitchen twine as tightly as possible.
- Wrap the results in plastic wrap and place the steak in the refrigerator before allowing it to marinate for at least an hour.
- Remove the plastic wrap before placing the steak on a baking sheet and placing the sheet in the oven for 35 minutes.
- Remove the string and broil for 10 minutes, rotating at the halfway point.

•Cover the baking sheet in foil and let it sit for 5 minutes prior to serving.

Kamut, Arugula and Orange Quinoa Salad

Total Prep & Cooking Time: 40 minutes

Yields: 6 Servings

Nutrition Facts (per serving)

- Protein: 2.8 g
- Carbs: 11.7 g
- Fats: 8.6 g
- Calories: 130

What to Use

- Shelled walnuts (.5 c roughly chopped)
- Kamut grains (1 c)
- Rocket Arugula (1 bunch)
- Pecorino Romano cheese ribbons (.5 c)
- Lemon juice (.5 lemons)
- Vegetable oil (1 tsp.)

- Water (2 c)
- Salt (1 tsp.)
- Blood oranges (2 medium, peeled, sliced cross-wise)
- Cold-pressed extra virgin olive oil (1 T)

Instructions:

- In a large bowl, place kamut in bowl with 4 c water and .5 lemon juice. Soak overnight.
- Rinse and strain kamut just before using.
- In the Instant Pot, add in strained Kamut together with salt, vegetable oil and 2 c water.
- Close and lock lid and cook on high till pot reaches pressure, then lower the heat to maintain least amount of pressure. Cook for 15 minutes.
- When beeper goes off, naturally release steam and open pot. Allow pressure to come down.
- In a serving bowl combine kamut, arugula, orange pieces, walnuts and olive oil.
- Combine all ingredients and drizzle Pecorino Romano ribbons. .25

Broccoli Soup

Total Prep & Cooking Time: 70 minutes

Yields: 5 Servings

Nutrition Facts (per serving)

- Protein: 11 g
- Carbs: 8 g
- Fats: 13 g
- Calories: 207

What to Use

- Butter (1 T)
- Onion (.5, white)
- Garlic (1 tsp, minced)
- Heavy cream (1.75 c plus 2 T)
- Broth (.5 c plus 2 T)
- Water (.5 c plus 2 T)
- Broccoli (1.5 c)
- Cheddar cheese (8 oz.)

- Salt and pepper (to taste)
- Paprika (.5 tsp)
- Xanthan Gum (.25 tsp)

Instructions:

- Chop up the onion and the broccoli.
- Add the butter to a large pot before placing it on top of a burner set to a medium heat.
- Sauté the onion with the garlic together for about 3 minutes.
- Mix in the water, cream, and the broth.   Bring to boil.
- Mix in the broccoli and the spices.
- Leave the pot be for 25 minutes.
- Add the cheese.
- Cool enough to put into the blender without shattering it.
- Add the gum and blend well.
- Pour into serving bowls.   Garnish with more cheddar cheese.

Chicken and shirataki noodles

Total Prep & Cooking Time: 20 minutes

Yields: 2 Servings

Nutrition Facts (per serving)

- Protein: 19.7 g

- Carbs: 6.2 g

- Fats: 17.2 g

- Calories: 323

What to use

- Black pepper (as desired)

- Chicken breast (.5 lbs. grilled)

- Coconut milk (.5 c)

- Shirataki noodles (.5 c)

- Water (2 c)

- Cheddar cheese (1 oz.)

Instructions:

- Add the shirataki noodles and the water to the instant pot cooker pot and seal the lid of the cooker. Choose the high-pressure option and set the time for 5 minutes.
- Once the timer goes off, select the instant pressure release option and switch the heat to sauté.
- Add in the cheese and coconut milk and stir until the cheese is melted.
- Plate the grilled chicken and top with cheese shirataki noodles prior to serving.

Grilled Shrimp

Total Prep & Cooking Time: 10 minutes

Yields: 2 Servings

Nutrition Facts (per serving)

- Protein: 32.5g
- Carbs: 1g
- Fat: 1.2g
- Calories: 159

Ingredients

- Shrimp (300g peeled)
- Dried dill (2 teaspoons)
- Paprika (2 teaspoons)
- 2 lemon wedges

Instructions:

- Place shrimp on skewers
- Season with lemon, dill and paprika
- Grill for 2 minutes on each side

Turkey and Onion Soup

Total Prep & Cooking Time: 1 hour 15 minutes

Yields: 4-6 Servings

Nutrition Facts (per serving)

- Protein: 93g
- Carbs: 14g
- Fat: 18g
- Calories: 629

Ingredients

- Boneless skineless turkey thighs (1lb diced)

- Fat-free chicken broth (2 cups)

- Water (2 cups)

- 1 bay leaf

- Garlic (3 cloves chopped)

- 1 scallion (sliced)

- 1 medium onion (diced)

- 3 large radishes (sliced)

- Dried spearmint (1 tablespoon)

- Dried basil (1 tablespoon)

Instructions:

- Place all ingredients in a large saucepan

- Bring to a boil for 5 minutes

- Turn down heat to simmer for 30-45 minutes then serve

High carb

Grecian Chicken Pasta

Total Prep & Cooking Time: 30 minutes

Yields: 6 Servings

Nutrition Facts (per serving)

- Protein: 32.6 g
- Carbs: 97 g
- Fats: 11.4 g
- Calories: 488

Ingredients

- Olive oil (1 T)
- Red onion (.5 c chopped)
- Linguine (16 oz.)
- Pepper (as desired)
- Salt (as desired)

- Lemons (2 wedged)
- Oregano (2 tsp. dried)
- Lemon juice (2 T)
- Parsley (3 T chopped)
- Feta cheese (.5 c crumbled)
- Tomato (1 chopped)
- Marinated artichoke hearts (14 oz. chopped, drained)
- Chicken breast (1 lb. cubed)
- Garlic (2 cloves crushed)

What to Do

- Fill a large pot with water and a pinch of salt before placing it on the stove on top of a burner that has been turned to a high heat. Once the water boils, add in the pasta and let it cook until it is still firm but just starting to become tender, which should take approximately 8 minutes.
- Add the olive oil to a skillet before placing it on top of a burner turned to a high/medium heat.

Place the garlic and onion into the skillet and let it cook for approximately 2 minutes until it begins to be fragrant.

White Beans, Tomatoes and Greek Pasta (vegetarian friendly)

Total Prep & Cooking Time: 25 minutes

Yields: 4 Servings

Nutrition Facts (per serving)

- Protein: 23.4 g
- Carbs: 109 g
- Fats: 5.9 g
- Calories: 460

What to Use

- Pepper (as desired)
- Salt (as desired)
- Feta cheese (.5 c crumbled)
- Penne pasta (8 oz.)
- Spinach (10 oz. chopped, washed)

- Cannellini beans (19 oz. rinsed, drained)
- Italian style tomatoes (14.5 oz. diced)

Instructions

- Fill a large pot with water and a pinch of salt before placing it on the stove on top of a burner that has been turned to a high heat. Once the water boils, add in the pasta and let it cook until it is just starting to become tender which should take about 8 minutes.
- While the pasta is cooking, add the olive oil to a skillet before placing it on top of a burner turned to a high/medium heat. Add in the beans and the tomatoes and let everything boil. After this occurs, reduce the heat to low/medium and let everything simmer for 10 minutes.
- Add in the spinach and let it cook for 2 minutes or until it starts to wilt, stirring regularly.
- Plate pasta and top with sauce and crumbled feta prior to serving.

- Mix in the chicken and stir regularly until the chicken ceases to be pink and all of its juices are clear, this should take approximately 5 minutes. The chicken should end up with an internal temperature of 165F.

- Turn the burner to a low/medium heat before adding in the pasta, oregano, lemon juice, parsley, feta cheese, tomato and artichoke hearts. Let the results cook while stirring for roughly 2 minutes.

Instant Pot Ribs With Creamy Coleslaw

Total Prep & Cooking Time: 67 minutes

Yields: 4 Servings

Nutrition Facts (per serving)

- Protein: 52 g
- Carbs: 96 g
- Fats: 88 g
- Calories: 780

What to Use - Ribs

- Chili powder (.5 tsp.)
- Baby back ribs (2 .5 lbs.)
- Salt (to taste)
- Paprika (.25 tsp.)
- Garlic powder (.3 tsp.)

What to Use - Sauce

- Tomato paste (8 oz.)
- Apple (.5 juiced)

- Bacon (2 slices cooked, crumbled)
- Onion (.5 c)
- Coconut oil (.25 c + 1 T)
- Paprika (.5 tsp)
- Black pepper (To taste)
- Salt (to taste)
- Ghee (1 T)
- Tomato sauce (.75 c)
- Garlic (1.5 cloves minced)
- Cayenne pepper (.3 tsp)
- Apple Cider vinegar (.5 c)

What to Use - Coleslaw

- Green organic cabbage (.5 heads shredded)
- Green onions (2 julienned)
- Red cabbage (.5 heads shredded)
- Raisins (1 c)
- Sweet mayonnaise (.6 c)
- Carrots (2 shredded)
- Organic ACV (.5 c)
- Celtic salt (as desired)

- Pepper (as desired)

Instructions - Coleslaw

- Combine the onions, carrots, cabbage, and raisins together in a medium-sized bowl.
- In another smaller one, mix well the mayonnaise, caraway seeds, and ACV and season as needed.
- Add the contents of the second bowl to the contents of the first and mix well. Cover and refrigerate till time to serve.
- To Make the Dry Rub
- To make the dry rub, mix onion powder, paprika, garlic powder, chili powder, pepper, salt and dry mustard.
- Cut the ribs into smaller slabs to fit into the Instant Cooker. Coat the ribs with the dry rub generously and place them into the pot.
- Add the minimum amount of water needed and insert the cooking rack. Place the ribs insides, loosely stacking them.

- Place the lid and seal it. Cook for 17 minutes, on high pressure.
- After 15 minutes is done and the ribs have cooked to perfection, allow for release the pressure naturally and then remove the lid.
- Move ribs to a clean plate, take out the cooking rack and discard any liquid from the pot.

Instructions - Sauce

- Click 'Sauté' to heat up the pot over low-pressure and add the bacon and cook until its crisp.
- Toss the garlic and the onion, sautéing for 5 minutes till onions have brown and are soft. Combine all the other items for the sauce and stir well to mix everything. Let simmer for another 10 minutes.
- Add ribs into the BBQ sauce and make sure to evenly coat so all the ribs are coated fully.
- Cook for an additional 10 minutes using a high pressure.
- Release valve to let go of pressure after 10 minutes and transfer ribs to serving dish.
- Serve ribs warm with a side of coleslaw.

Snacks & Desserts

Low carb

Orangesicle smoothie

Total Prep & Cooking Time: 5 minutes

Yields: 1 Serving

Nutrition Facts (per serving)

Net Carbs: 7 g

Protein: 8 g

Fats: 12 g

Calories: 328

What to Use

- Ice cubes (6)
- Your choice of sweetener (to taste)
- Coconut milk (.75 c)
- Vanilla whey protein (1 scoop)

- Coconut oil (2 T)
- Plain skyr (2 oz.)
- Fresh orange juice (8 oz.)
- Carrot (2 oz. shredded)
- Mango (1 ripe)

Instructions

- Cream the coconut milk: This is a simple process. All you need to do is place the can of coconut milk in the refrigerator overnight. The next morning, open the can and spoon out the coconut milk that has solidified. Don't shake the can before opening. Discard the liquids.
- Add all of the ingredients, save the ice cubes, to the blender and blend on a low speed until pureed. Thin with water as needed.
- Add in the ice cubes and blend until the smoothie reaches your desired consistency.

Roasted brussels sprouts

Total Prep & Cooking Time: 60 minutes

Yields: 6 Servings

Nutrition Facts (per serving)

- Protein: 2.9 g
- Carbs: 10 g
- Fats: 7.3 g
- Calories: 104

What to Use

- Black pepper (as desired)
- Sea salt (as desired)
- Olive oil (3 T)
- Brussels sprouts (1.5 lbs.)

Instructions

- Ensure your oven is set to 400F.

- Add the oil, salt, pepper and brussels sprouts into a large Ziploc bag before sealing the bag tightly and shaking well to ensure the brussels sprouts are well coated.

- Add the sprouts to a baking sheet and place the sheet on the center oven rack for 35 minutes, taking care to shake regularly to guarantee even browning. You will be able to tell that the brussels sprouts are ready when they are such a dark brown that they are almost black.

Coconut Cream Macaroons

Total Prep & Cooking Time: 70 minutes

Yields: 5 Servings

Nutrition Facts (per serving)

Protein: 6 g

Carbs: 2 g

Fat: 12 g

Calories: 78

What to Use

- Heavy cream (3 ounces)
- Cream cheese (9 ounces)
- Vanilla (1 tsp.)
- Egg whites (4 or 5)
- Cream of tartar (.25 tsp.)
- Erythritol (1 cup)
- Salt (.125 tsp.)
- Dried coconut (18 ounces)

- Unsweetened white chocolate syrup (to taste)
- Semi-sweet chocolate chips (to taste)

Instructions

- Preheat oven to 325 degrees Fahrenheit.
- Separate the yolks from the eggs.
- Whisk the egg whites, vanilla, cream of tartar, and the salt together, occasionally sprinkling in the erythritol.   Whisk until the mixture peaks.
- Add coconut to the egg white mixture.   Mix and set bowl aside.
- In a separate bowl, mix together the chocolate syrup, cream cheese, and the heavy cream. Mix ingredients well.
- Add the ingredients from the other bowl and mix all the ingredients together.
- Add the chocolate chips after everything else is mixed.   Scoop mixture onto a cookie sheet. Bake in preheated oven for about 25 minutes. Turn the oven off and let the cookies remain in the oven another 30 minutes, so they will dry.

Cottage Cheese and Grapefruit Protein Bowl

Total Prep & Cooking Time: 5 minutes

Yields: 1 Serving

Nutrition Facts (per serving)

- Protein: 34 g
- Carbs: 10 g
- Fat: 1 g
- Calories: 180 calories

Ingredients

- Red grapefruit (80g diced)
- 2 grams sucralose
- Fat free cottage cheese (200g)
- Vanilla Extract (1/4 teaspoon, 2 drops)

Instructions
- Combine ingredients together in a bowl and serve

High Carb

Banana and Peanut Butter Smoothie

Total Prep & Cooking Time: 5 minutes

Yields: 1 Servings

Nutrition Facts (per serving)

- Calories: 466
- Protein: 18 g
- Carbohydrates 60 g
- Fat: 16.5 g

What to Use

- Ice cubes (6)
- Banana (1)
- Unsalted peanut butter (3 T)
- Palin yogurt (.5 c fat free)
- Milk (.5 cup fat free)

Instructions

- Add all of the ingredients to a blender and blend until smooth.
- Serve chilled, does not keep well.

Vanilla Lasagna

Total Prep & Cooking Time: 60 minutes

Yields: 8 Servings

Nutrition Facts (per serving)

Protein: 6.5g

Carbs: 65 g

Fat: 18.5g

Calories: 345

What to Use

- Vanilla pudding (4 single-serving containers)
- Honey graham crackers (1 box)
- Fat-free whipped cream (13 oz.)
- Mini chocolate chip morsels (1 c)

Instructions

- Empty the vanilla pudding packs into a mixing bowl.
- Place three c of whipped cream into the bowl of pudding.
- Cover the bottom of a baking pan in graham crackers.
- Spread half of the pudding mixture on top of graham crackers.
- Add another layer of graham cracker.
- Spread the other half of pudding mixture on top of graham crackers.
- Add a final layer of graham cracker.
- Chill.
- Upon removing from the refrigerator and prior to serving, spray the top of dessert with remaining whipped topping then sprinkle 1 cup of mini chocolate chip morsels over top of dessert.

Peanut Butter Rice Bars

Total Prep & Cooking Time: 55minutes

Yields: 3 Servings

Nutrition Facts (per serving)

- Protein: 12 g (37g with protein powder)

- Carbohydrates 50 g

- Fat: 16 g

- Calories: 168 (268 with protein powder)

What to Use

- Maple Syrup (2 T)
- Rice (2 cups cooked)
- Peanut butter (.25 c)
- Optional: 1 scoop protein powder of your choice

Instructions

- Place the peanut butter into a microwavable bowl and heat it in the microwave for 45 seconds.
- In a small bowl, mix together the rice, maple syrup and peanut butter and mix thoroughly.
- Add the results to a glass container (8x8) and place in the refrigerator to harden.
- It is best to eat the resulting bars quickly as they will melt if left unattended for too long.

What to Do When Your

Weight Loss Stalls

Congratulations, if this chapter is relevant to you then it means your fat loss journey has been a success so far, so props to you for that.

You've been hitting your macro goals on the daily, lifting weights, and most importantly, had fun doing so.

But now your fat loss has slowed down, maybe you've hit a plateau, so what to do next?

One of the more important elements of a long-term carb cycling plan is your **refeed day**. This is a day when you replenish your glycogen stores in your muscle by eating larger amounts of carbs than normal.

Refeed days also have mental benefits, because they act as a "break" from your diet. Notice that I use the word refeed as opposed to "cheat day", this is because a refeed is more of a scientific approach as opposed to the traditional cheat day that seems to have been glorified in the past few years (especially in the YouTube fitness community where it has become equivalent to binge eating).

Generally, the leaner you get, the more frequent you will need a refeed day. If you're above 20% body fat then you should only need one once in a blue moon. Once you hit the 15% for men (25% for women) then you will start needing to incorporate them more regularly.

As a general rule of thumb (add 10% body fat) for women:

Above 15-20% body fat: refeed once 2 weeks.

10-15%~ body fat: refeed once a week.

Less than 10% body fat: refeed twice per week.

Note, if you are still losing weight, do not refeed and stay on your regular diet.

How to structure your refeed day

Instead of just going all out and hitting every buffet in town (as tempting as that may be), then I recommend lowering your protein and fat intake by 20g each and then doubling your carb intake for the day. For example, if your average carb intake is 250g a day, then you can have 500g for the day. If you are under 10% bodyfat then increase carbs by 50% to counteract the fact you're doing this every 3 or 4 days.

Yes, this is a lot, you don't have to hit that target, but if you are eating junk food (like a large pizza for example) then it's likely you'll hit it anyway. I'm not going to give you a list of foods you can and can't eat on this day, too much diet and recipe books preach too heavily on that front. Just enjoy yourself, make sure you get enough fiber and micronutrients and drink a lot of water. The only thing I will say is to try not to consume too many foods high in fructose on your refeed day (the big culprits are low fat salad dressing, syrups, cereals, sodas and pickles). This is because fructose has an adverse effect on your leptin levels.

Conclusion

Thank you for reading *Carb Cycling Recipes: Fat Shredding, Muscle Building Meals Which Will Eliminate Your Skinnyfat Physique Forever*. I hope it was informative and able to provide you with all of the tools you need to achieve your goals whatever they may be.

Now that you've read this book you are equipped to take steps toward your fat loss goals, whatever they may be. You've seen the science, now its time to apply it. Focus on your weight loss goals and stick to your target calorie intake while going to the gym, and you really can't fail. A lot of people tend to overcomplicate diets and weight loss routines, but just keep going one day at a time and you are destined to succeed.

When it comes to your workout routine, remember that you don't need to compare yourself to anyone else. Just because that fitness "model" on Instagram takes incredible pictures and looks great from certain angles, doesn't mean that they didn't have to take 1000 photos to get there. **Don't compare your behind the scenes to anyone else's highlight reel.** Your only competition in your fat loss journey is yourself.

Don't worry if you have a week where the scale doesn't move, that's completely normal in a sustained fat loss plan. Just incorporate refeed days when appropriate and you will be back on track sooner than you think. One last thing, don't look at yourself in the mirror every day (unless you're competing for a bodybuilding or fitness show), doing so will probably have a negative effect on your fitness goals. Instead, take a before picture, and compare yourself to that. If you look better (and you will), then you are clearly doing something right.

Most importantly, enjoy yourself. This book was designed as a solution for those who often struggle with weight loss in general. The diet plan was scheduled to be as simple as possible while still being effective, and I hope you find that is the case.

Finally, if you found this book useful in any way, a review on Amazon is always appreciated!

Yours in health,

Jason Michaels

Other Books by Jason

Michaels

Anti-Inflammatory Diet: Make these simple, inexpensive changes to your diet and start feeling better within 24 hours!

Anti-Inflammatory Diet: The Complete Guide for Managing Rheumatoid Arthritis and Healing Chronic Disease Using Healthy Food

Keto Meal Prep: How to Save $100 and 4 Hours A Week by Batch Cooking

17275037R00057

Printed in Great Britain
by Amazon